PivotTables
Easy Excel Essentials
Volume 1

M.L. HUMPHREY

Copyright © 2017-2018 M.L. Humphrey

All rights reserved.

ISBN: 1720561532
ISBN-13: 978-1720561538

TITLES BY M.L. HUMPHREY

EASY EXCEL ESSENTIALS
Pivot Tables
Conditional Formatting
Charts
The IF Functions
Formatting
Printing

EXCEL ESSENTIALS
Excel for Beginners
Intermediate Excel
50 Useful Excel Functions
50 More Excel Functions

EXCEL ESSENTIALS QUIZ BOOKS
The Excel for Beginners Quiz Book
The Intermediate Excel Quiz Book
The 50 Useful Excel Functions Quiz Book
The 50 More Excel Functions Quiz Book

DATA PRINCIPLES
Data Principles for Beginners

BUDGETING FOR BEGINNERS
Budgeting for Beginners
Excel for Budgeting

WORD ESSENTIALS
Word for Beginners
Intermediate Word

MAIL MERGE
Mail Merge for Beginners

POWERPOINT ESSENTIALS
PowerPoint for Beginners

CONTENTS

Introduction	1
Pivot Tables	3
Conclusion	21
Appendix: Basic Terminology	23

INTRODUCTION

In *Excel for Beginners* I covered the basics of working in Excel, including how to format in Excel and how to print. In *Intermediate Excel* I covered a number of intermediate-level topics such as pivot tables, charts, and conditional formatting. And in *50 Useful Excel Functions* I covered fifty of the most useful functions you can use in Excel.

But I realize that some users will just want to know about a specific topic and not buy a guide that covers a variety of other topics that aren't of interest to them.

So this series of guides is meant to address that need. Each guide in the series covers one specific topic such as pivot tables, conditional formatting, or charts.

I'm going to assume in these guides that you have a basic understanding of how to navigate Excel, although each guide does include an Appendix with a brief discussion of basic terminology to make sure that we're on the same page.

The guides are written using Excel 2013, which should be similar enough for most users of Excel to follow, but anyone using a version of Excel prior to Excel 2007 probably won't be able to use them effectively.

Also, keep in mind that the content in these guides is drawn from *Excel for Beginners, Intermediate Excel,* and/or *50 Useful Excel Functions*, so if you think you'll end up buying more than one or two of these guides you're probably better off just buying *Excel for Beginners, Intermediate Excel,* and/or *50 Useful Excel Functions*.

With that said, let's talk Pivot Tables.

PIVOT TABLES

A pivot table takes rows and rows of data and puts it into nice summary reports based on the criteria you set. I use these all the time.

They're great for summarizing the Amazon daily and monthly sales reports for book sales that I use as a publisher. In less than a minute I can see what sales I have by title or how much I've earned in each currency or how many page reads I've had. I also use it to see my ad spend by title, month, or author.

Pivot tables can be used on any listing of data where you have more than one entry per customer or product or whatever it is you want to analyze. So say you run a small business and had 1,000 sales this year and now you want to know who your best customer was and all you have is those 1,000 entries. You could sort by customer and then manually add up sales for each one, which could take hours. (Or use subtotals.)

The better option, though, is to create a pivot table that calculates total sales for each customer and then to sort that table to see who's at the top. You'll be done in less than five minutes.

Sounds great, right?

So how do they work? What do you do?

First, you need your information organized in the right format. There needs to be one row that contains the labels for each column. (I sometimes call this the header row.) Directly below that you need to list your information with one row per entry and nothing else other than the data.

The mistake a lot of people make (and Amazon used to do this with their monthly reports) is that they'll list information in one row and then below that row list a subset of information. So maybe Row 5 is the customer information and then below that they list the transactions for that customer in Rows 6-10 and then Row 11 is another row of customer information and below that are the transactions for the customer in Row 11.

The problem with that approach is that you can't easily manipulate that data. You can't sort it, filtering it is a challenge, you can't use pivot tables with it, and you can't create charts from it either.

It's information that's there for display purposes not analysis.

Don't do that.

At least not in your source worksheet.

Always have one place where you simply list your information. You can then use that worksheet to create summary reports and do any data analysis you need to do, but always have one location where you list just your data and nothing else.

Also try not to have any blank rows or columns in your dataset and try to have only one type of data (date, currency, text) per column.

(Blank rows aren't a deal-breaker, but Excel will treat them as valid sources of data so you'll end up with blank entries in your summary tables. Blank columns will generate an error message when you try to create the pivot table.)

To understand the proper way to display your data, let's look at an example:

EASY EXCEL ESSENTIALS: PIVOT TABLES

	A	B	C	D
1	Albert Jones			
2		8/1/2015	1 widget, 1 other	$25.00
3		8/30/2015	10 widgets	$250.00
4		9/1/2015	3 whatchamacallits	$45.00
5				
6	Richard Martinez			
7		3/7/2016	10 who knows what	$35.00
8		4/7/2016	20 whatsits	$30.00

Bad Data Layout

Customer	Date of Transaction	Quantity	Item	Unit Price	Total
Albert Jones	8/1/2015	1	Widget	$ 20.00	$ 20.00
Albert Jones	8/1/2015	1	Other	$ 5.00	$ 5.00
Albert Jones	8/30/2015	10	Widget	$ 25.00	$ 250.00
Albert Jones	9/1/2015	3	Whatchamacallit	$ 15.00	$ 45.00
Richard Martinez	3/7/2016	10	Who knows what	$ 3.50	$ 35.00
Richard Martinez	4/7/2016	20	Whasit	$ 1.50	$ 30.00

Good Data Layout

On the top is a display of information that you can't do anything with. Look at customer Albert Jones. How many units has he bought total? How many widgets vs. whatchamacallits? And overall, how many widgets have you sold this year? And to whom? You'd have to physically calculate those numbers because of the way they were recorded. (This is fine for a final report, but it shouldn't be how you store that information initially.)

In contrast, look at the bottom example. It's the same information. But now if we want to know how many widgets Mr. Jones has bought we can just filter that list by customer and widget. (Or we can create a pivot table which we'll do in a moment.) Same with overall number of units sold for the year. Just add a quick formula and you have your answer.

So what are the rules? How should you structure your data to get the most use out of it?

1. Use the first row of your worksheet to label your data.
2. List all of your data in continuous rows after that first row without including any subtotals or subheadings or anything that isn't your data.
3. To the extent possible, format your data in such a way that it can be analyzed. (So rather than put in a free-text field, try to use a standardized list of values instead. For example, a 1 to 5 point ranking scale instead of a free text field.)
4. Standardize your values. Customer A should always be listed as Customer A. United States should always be United States not USA, U.S.A., or America.
5. Store your raw data in one location; analyze or correct it elsewhere.
6. Have a separate column for anything you might want to analyze. (So don't have "1 blue widget" instead have columns for quantity, color, and product.)

This may mean you repeat information, such as customer name in multiple rows.

That's fine.

(Just be sure it's standardized and Customer A is always written the same way.)

The analysis you can perform depends one hundred percent on how you structure your data.

Okay then. Assuming you have a good set of data to work with, it's time to create a pivot table.

Highlight your data. (If it's the entire worksheet, you can Select All by clicking in the top left corner. If the data starts lower down in the worksheet, be sure to highlight the header row as well as the data rows.)

Next, go to the Insert tab and choose Pivot Table.

EASY EXCEL ESSENTIALS: PIVOT TABLES

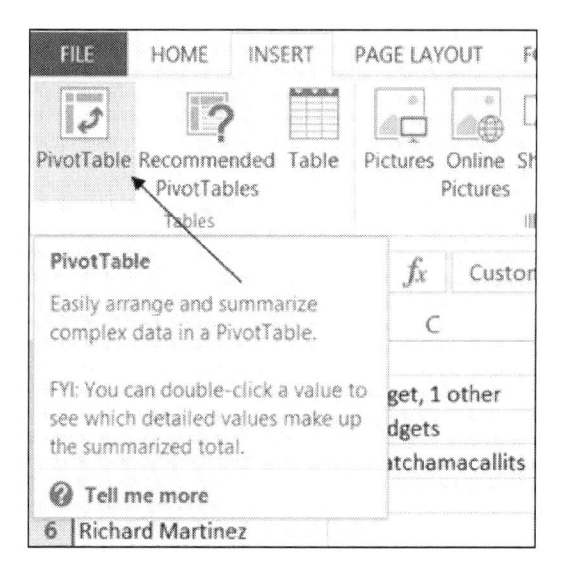

Choose to add your Pivot Table to a new worksheet.

(I always do this because I don't want my source data and my pivot table to interfere with one another.)

After you do so, you should see a blank pivot table on the left-hand side and a listing of the available pivot table fields on the right-hand side.

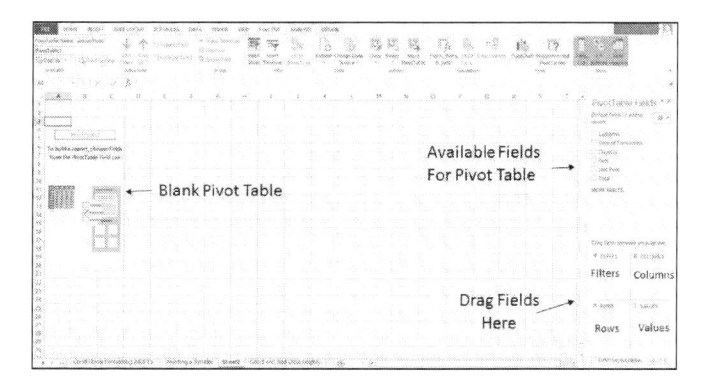

Click on the name of each of the fields you want to use and either drag each field to the table on the left or to the area in the bottom right corner where it says "Drag fields between areas below." I prefer to drag them downward, but both ways work.

If you want the values in a field listed down the left-hand side of your column use Rows.

If you want the values in a field listed across the top of your table use Columns.

For any values that you want to calculate, such as quantity, amount earned, etc. place that field in the Values section of the Pivot Table.

And if you want to be able to filter on a value, place that field in the Filters section.

In this example I dragged Customer to the Rows section and Quantity and Total to the Values section. This gave me a pivot table where I could see quantity bought and total paid by customer.

	A	B	C
1			
2			
3	Row Labels	Sum of Quantity	Sum of Total
4	Albert Jones	15	320
5	Richard Martinez	30	65
6	**Grand Total**	**45**	**385**
7			

For any field you drag to the Values section, be sure that the correct function is being performed on the data.

I have some datasets (Amazon's) that I work with where the default is to Count numbers instead of Sum them.

To change the function being performed on the data, click on the arrow next to the field name and choose Value Field Settings.

EASY EXCEL ESSENTIALS: PIVOT TABLES

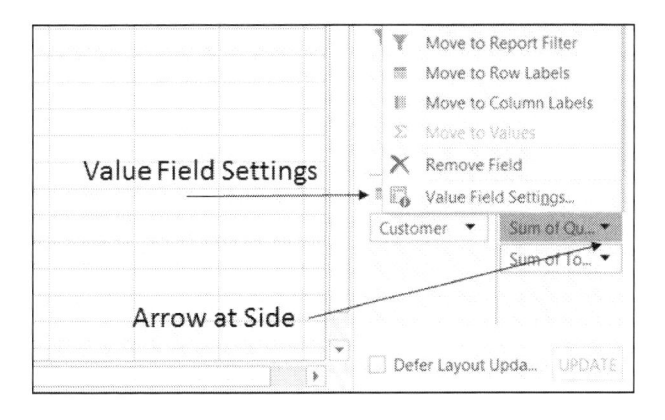

This will bring up the Value Field Settings dialogue box where you can choose to display the results as a Sum, Count, Average, Minimum, Maximum, Product, Count Numbers, or Standard Deviation. You can also choose on the Show Values As tab to show the result as a % of the Grand Total, % of the Column Total, % of the Row Total, as well as a number of other options.

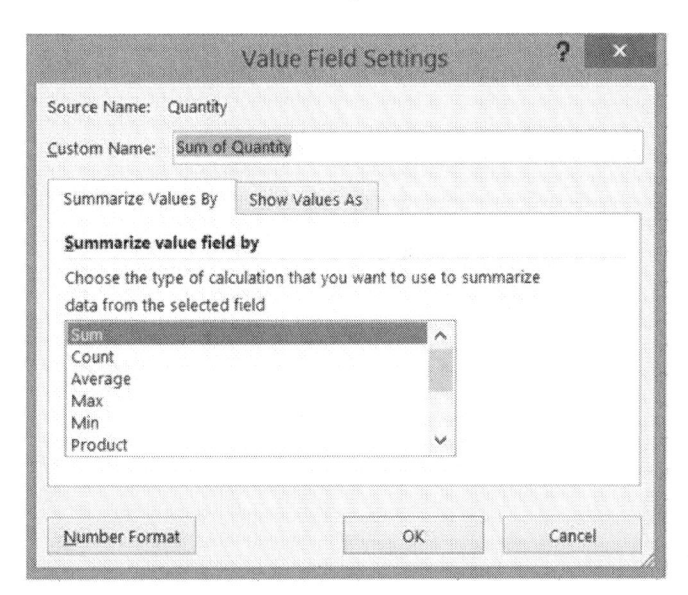

In the Value Field Settings dialogue box you can also choose how to format the values in that column of the table by clicking on the Number Format box at the bottom.

(You can also format the cells by highlighting them and using the Number section of the Home tab to choose your format or by highlighting them, right-clicking, and choosing Format Cells.)

If you want to perform two (or more) calculations with the same field, just add it more than once and specify for each instance the function you want performed.

You can also add variables to go across the top of the table as well.

Below I've added Item into the Columns section of the pivot table.

Since I had two entries listed in the Values section, it creates two columns for each Item.

EASY EXCEL ESSENTIALS: PIVOT TABLES

	A	B	C	D
1			First Item	
2				
3		Column Labels		
4		Other		Whasit
5	Row Labels	Sum of Quantity	Sum of Total	Sum of Qua
6	Albert Jones		1	$5.00
7	Richard Martinez			
8	Grand Total		1	$5.00
9				
10				
11			Values for	
12				
13			First Item	
14				

If you don't like the order that your entries are in, you can right-click on an entry and use the Move option to change the display order. You can do this within the values for each variable (so I could move Other to the end in the above example) or when you have multiple column or row variables.

If I remove Unit Price from Values, then it's a much simpler table to view.

Here we have Item across the top, customer down the side, and the units of each item bought by each customer in the table:

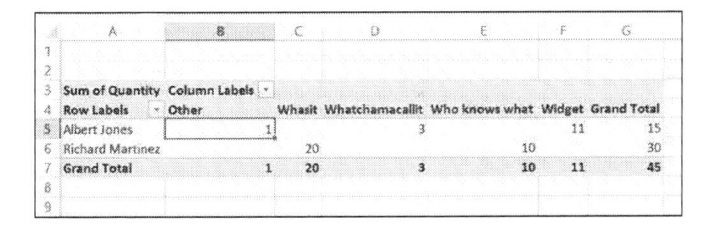

	A	B	C	D	E	F	G
1							
2							
3	Sum of Quantity	Column Labels					
4	Row Labels	Other	Whasit	Whatchamacallit	Who knows what	Widget	Grand Total
5	Albert Jones	1		3		11	15
6	Richard Martinez		20		10		30
7	Grand Total	1	20	3	10	11	45
8							
9							

You can also filter the results in your pivot table so that it's specific to a subset of your data.

To apply a filter, you move the field you want to filter by into the Filters section and then choose the values you want from the drop down menu. Uncheck any values you don't want included in the table.

For example, here I moved Item to the Filters section and then unchecked all items except Whatchamacallits. (The easy way to do this is click the box next to (All) so that all values are unselected and then choose the one you want.)

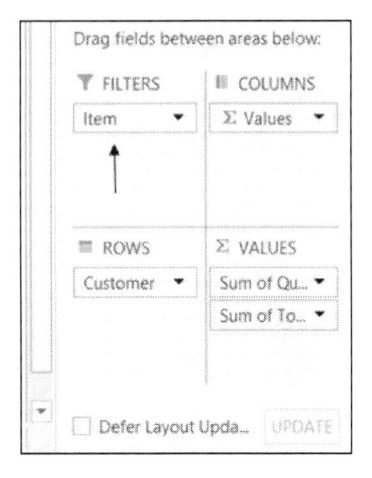

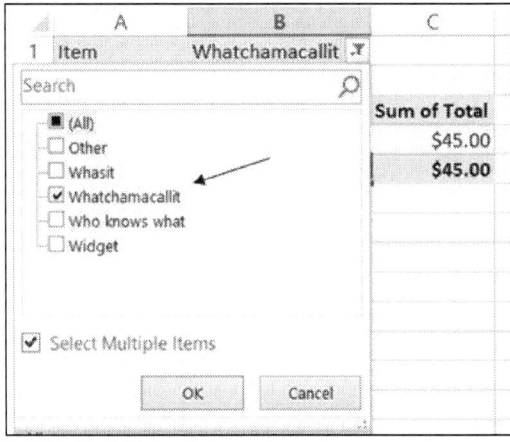

There are a number of other things you can do with pivot tables using the Analyze tab under PivotTable Tools. (If you aren't seeing PivotTable Tools, click on the pivot table in the worksheet.)

EASY EXCEL ESSENTIALS: PIVOT TABLES

* * *

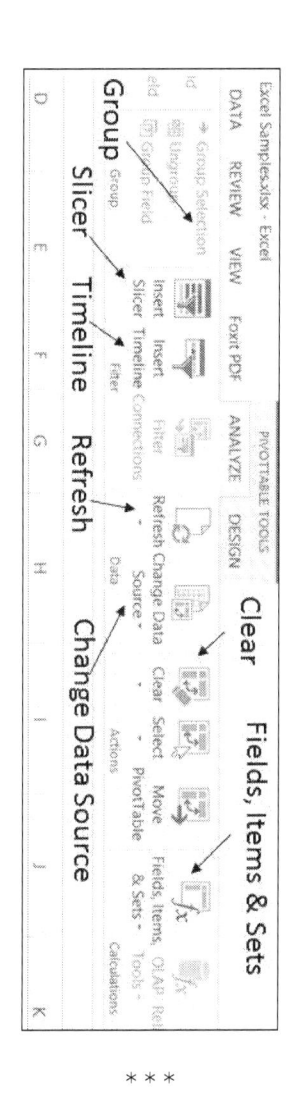

You can create an artificial grouping of entries by clicking on each of the items you want to include in the group while holding down the Ctrl key and then choosing Group

Selection from the Group section of the Analyze tab. To remove a grouping, click on the Group name and then choose Ungroup.

Once you've grouped a set of results (say books in a series or related customer accounts), you can click on the minus sign next to the group name and that will hide the individual entries that make up that group and only display the totals for the group.

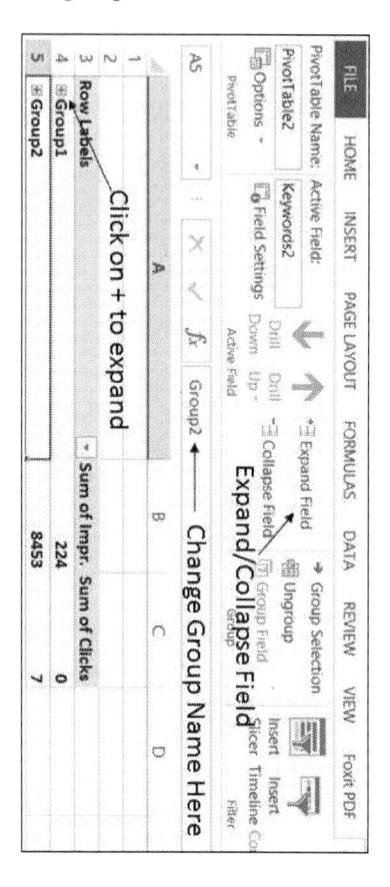

To rename a group, click on its name and then change the group name in the formula bar.

Clicking on Collapse Field in the Active Field section of the Analyze tab will collapse all grouped entries into their summary row. Clicking on Expand Field will expand all of them.

* * *

I've never used Insert Slicer before, but it seems to basically work like a filter option, without being a filter. So you can choose to insert a slicer, click on the field you want to slice by, and then click on the values for that field that appear in the slicer box and it will narrow your pivot table down to just the results that match that criteria. To undo your slice, click on the funnel image in the top right corner of that box.

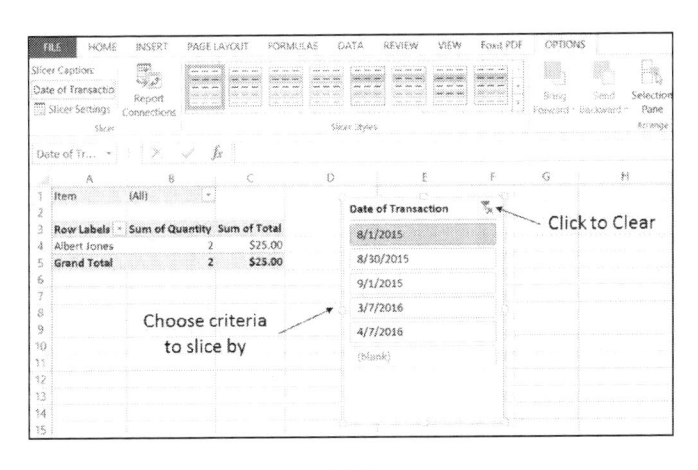

* * *

Insert Timeline is another one I've never used before. It appears to use any date provided in your data and let you narrow it down by month, quarter, year, or day. This is very handy for data where you have just the date (8/9/15) but want to see the data by month or year without having to add new fields to your original data source. (And certainly beats my old method of filtering by date and then checking/unchecking boxes.)

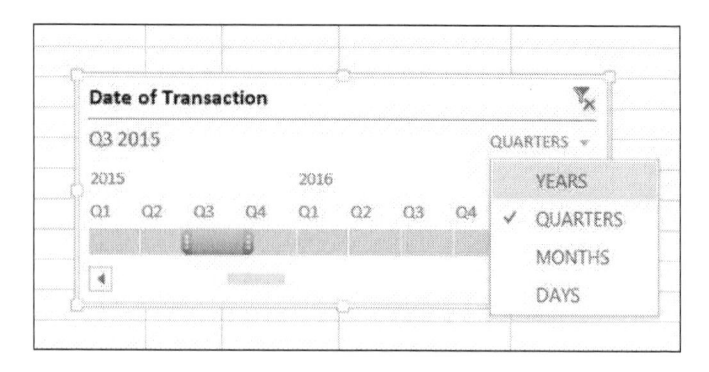

***

You can use Refresh to update the table if your source data changes. For example, you might find that customer Albert Jones was entered as Albert Jones and Albert R. Jones so is showing as two different entries. After you go back to your source data and update one of the entries, click on Refresh to have Excel regenerate the table to reflect the change.

***

You can also use Change Data Source to change the data the pivot table includes. For example, if you've added additional entries since it was last generated. Click on Change Data Source and then Change Data Source in the dropdown menu and it will take you to the page with your source data as well as highlight the cells contained in that range.

The easiest way to update the range is to use your cursor to select all of the cells you want in range. If you have thousands of rows of data, you can select the top section of the data and then click into the box and change the final number to correspond to the last row of your data. (If you try just updating the cell references by typing in the data field, it sometimes gets messed up and tries adding cell ranges within your existing range, so I usually avoid that approach.)

* * *

If you want to keep the pivot table but start over fresh by removing all fields and settings, you can click on Clear, and choose Clear All. To clear just the filters you've applied to the table, click on Clear and choose Clear Filters.

* * *

If you want to add a new calculation to the table (for example, I usually want to place a dollar value on my page reads which requires multiplying them by a constant), you can do so using Fields, Items, & Sets.

Click on it and choose Calculated Field. You'll see a dialogue box where you can name the field and build a calculation using existing fields and/or other numbers.

Here I've calculated a tax due amount using a 5.75% tax rate:

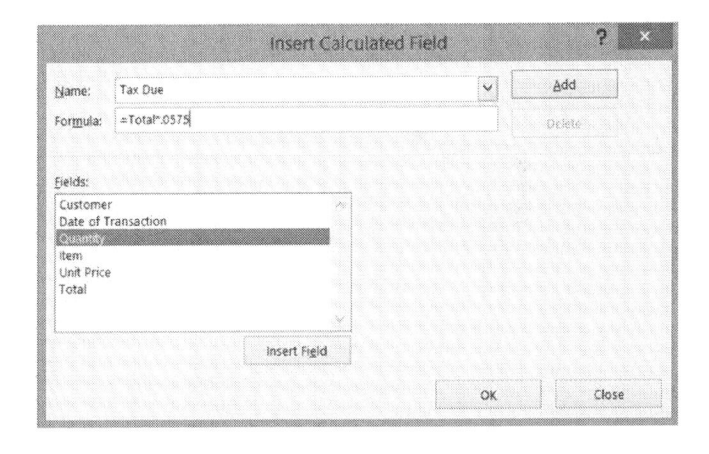

![Insert Calculated Field dialogue box with Name: Tax Due, Formula: =Total*.0575, Fields list: Customer, Date of Transaction, Quantity, Item, Unit Price, Total]

When you're done, click on OK. The field should be listed

in your Pivot Table Fields and may already be shown in your table. If it isn't showing in your table, drag it to where you want it to be and change any value field settings you need to change.

(So that, for example, it sums the values instead of counts them.)

* * *

The Design tab under Pivot Table Tools allows you to choose how the table displays. You can change the color, add a blank row after every entry in the table, choose when and how to display subtotals, choose when and how to display grand totals, and change the formatting of the row and column headers.

It basically allows you a number of options to refine your table results to display according to your preferences. For example, in the image on the next page I've chosen to change the color, add a line between entries, display the column grand totals, not display subtotals or row totals, and I've kept the row and column headers bolded.

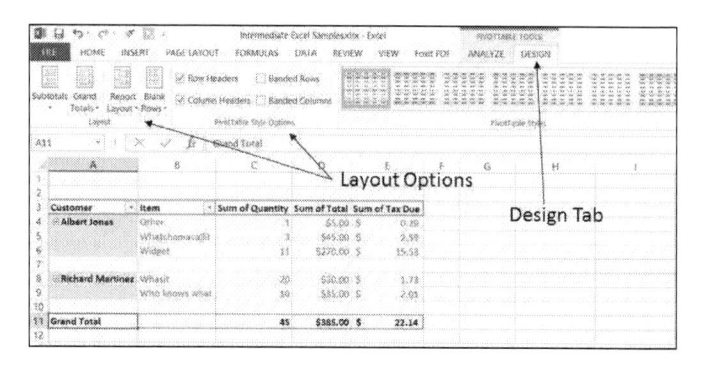

* * *

What else?

To remove a field you didn't want to add to the table, click on the arrow next to the field name in the field grid in the bottom right corner of the worksheet and choose Remove Field.

You can also right-click in a cell in a column in the table and choose Remove [Column] to remove a column from the table. Or right-click on a row value and choose Remove [Row] to remove a row from the table. (I use brackets there because the option will actually name the row or column you're allowed to delete. So, it'll say "Remove Units" for the Units variable.)

If you have multiple entries under Row, Column, or Values and want to change their order, left-click and drag the field to where you want it.

To undo something you just did and didn't like, click anywhere in the worksheet and use Ctrl + Z. (It won't work until you've clicked into the worksheet for whatever strange reason.)

One thing to be cautious of when working with pivot tables is that they're dynamic. The number of rows is not set and the number of columns can easily change based upon your choices of what to include or not include in the table.

This is the reason I tend to build them as I need them but not keep them long-term. If you do set one up that you want to repeatedly run, which I can see doing if you get fancy with your settings, just be careful that (a) you always have all the data you want to include selected and (b) that you don't add other text or calculations around the table that could be overwritten or become inaccurate when the table is refreshed.

(You'll see if you try to write a formula referencing an entry in a pivot table that it isn't just referencing that cell, it's instead referencing the pivot table and an entire subset of the data in the table based upon the listed criteria. So you might write a formula in Row 6 that corresponds to Customer Jones who is currently listed in Row 6 but then refresh your table and Customer Jones is now in Row 8 but the formula is still in Row 6 and still refers to Customer Jones.)

My advice if you want to do additional calculations on your data is to either copy the entire table and paste special-values and then do your analysis on that pasted table, or to build the calculations into the table itself as discussed above. Don't mix the two. Don't create a pivot table and then do external computations on those values while it's still a pivot table.

Alright.

Hopefully that was a good, solid beginning with respect to pivot tables. The big topic I didn't cover here is how to link multiple tables of data to create one pivot table, which is a more advanced use of the tables than 99% of people will ever need.

CONCLUSION

So that was pivot tables, probably the single most useful tool in Excel. (Some might argue for VLOOKUP, but on a day-to-day basis I know that I at least am far more likely to use a pivot table than VLOOKUP or, what I use instead, nested IF functions.)

Remember that the format of your data is crucial to your ability to use a Pivot Table. And don't forget to keep your raw data safe in one location while analyzing it in another. This isn't as much of an issue with pivot tables as it is with sorting or some of the other irreversible steps you can take with Excel, but it's always a good habit to get into.

And don't forget to gut check any results your pivot table analysis provides. It's rare but I have had the occasional situation where the pivot table failed to capture all of my entries and so my grand total wasn't what I knew it should be.

Good luck with it, and reach out if you have questions or get stuck.

APPENDIX A: BASIC TERMINOLOGY

Column

Excel uses columns and rows to display information. Columns run across the top of the worksheet and, unless you've done something funky with your settings, are identified using letters of the alphabet.

Row

Rows run down the side of the worksheet and are numbered starting at 1 and up to a very high number.

Cell

A cell is a combination of a column and row that is identified by the letter of the column it's in and the number of the row it's in. For example, Cell A1 is the cell in the first column and first row of a worksheet.

Click

If I tell you to click on something, that means to use your mouse (or trackpad) to move the arrow on the screen over to a specific location and left-click or right-click on the option. (See the next definition for the difference between left-click and right-click).

If you left-click, this selects the item. If you right-click, this generally creates a dropdown list of options to choose from. If I don't tell you which to do, left- or right-click, then left-click.

Left-click/Right-click

If you look at your mouse or your trackpad, you generally have two flat buttons to press. One is on the left side, one is on the right. If I say left-click that means to press down on the button on the left. If I say right-click that means press down on the button on the right. (If you're used to using Word or Excel you may already do this without even thinking about it. So, if that's the case then think of left-click as what you usually use to select text and right-click as what you use to see a menu of choices.)

Spreadsheet

I'll try to avoid using this term, but if I do use it, I'll mean your entire Excel file. It's a little confusing because it can sometimes also be used to mean a specific worksheet, which is why I'll try to avoid it as much as possible.

Worksheet

This is the term I'll use as much as possible. A worksheet is a combination of rows and columns that you can enter data in. When you open an Excel file, it opens to worksheet one.

Formula Bar

This is the long white bar at the top of the screen with the $f\chi$ symbol next to it.

Tab

I refer to the menu choices at the top of the screen (File, Home, Insert, Page Layout, Formulas, Data, Review, and View) as tabs. Note how they look like folder tabs from an old-time filing system when selected? That's why.

Data

I use data and information interchangeably. Whatever information you put into a worksheet is your data.

Select

If I tell you to "select" cells, that means to highlight them.

Arrow

If I say that you can "arrow" to something that just means to use the arrow keys to navigate from one cell to another.

A1:A25

If I'm going to reference a range of cells, I'll use the shorthand notation that Excel uses in its formulas. So, for example, A1:A25 will mean Cells A1 through A25. If you ever don't understand exactly what I'm referring to, you can type it into a cell in Excel using the = sign and see what cells Excel highlights. So, =A1:A25 should highlight cells A1 through A25 and =A1:B25 should highlight the cells in columns A and B and rows 1 through 25.

With Formulas Visible

Normally Excel doesn't show you the formula in a cell unless you click on that cell and then you only see the formula in the formula bar. But to help you see what I'm referring to, some of the screenshots in this guide will be provided with formulas visible. All this means is that I clicked on Show Formulas on the Formulas tab so that you could see what cells have formulas in them and what those formulas are.

Unless you do the same, your worksheet will not look like that. That's okay. Because you don't need to have your formulas visible unless you're troubleshooting something that isn't working.

Dialogue Box

I will sometimes reference a dialogue box. These are the boxes that occasionally pop up with additional options for you to choose from for that particular task. Usually I include a screen shot so you know what it should look like.

Paste Special – Values

I will sometimes suggest that you paste special-values. What this means is to paste your data using the Values option under Paste Options (the one with 123 on the clipboard). This will paste the values from the cells you copied without also bringing over any of the formulas that created those values.

Dropdown

I will occasionally refer to a dropdown or dropdown menu. This is generally a list of potential choices that you can select from. The existence of the list is indicated by an arrow next to the first available selection. I will occasionally refer to the list of options you see when you click on a dropdown arrow as the dropdown menu.

ABOUT THE AUTHOR

M.L. Humphrey is a former stockbroker with a degree in Economics from Stanford and an MBA from Wharton who has spent close to twenty years as a regulator and consultant in the financial services industry.

You can reach M.L. at mlhumphreywriter@gmail.com or at mlhumphrey.com.

Printed in Poland
by Amazon Fulfillment
Poland Sp. z o.o., Wrocław